r a-t

THE SHEARSMAN CHAPBOOK SERIES, 2014

Martyn Crucefix *The Time We Turned*
Patricia Debney *Gestation*
juli Jana *ra-t*
Anthony Rudolf *Go into the Question*
Robert Vas Dias *Arrivals and Departures*

r
  a
   -t

juli Jana

Shearsman Books

First published in the United Kingdom in 2014 by
Shearsman Books
50 Westons Hill Drive
Emersons Green
BRISTOL
BS16 7DF

Shearsman Books Ltd Registered Office
30–31 St. James Place, Mangotsfield, Bristol BS16 9JB
(this address not for correspondence)

www.shearsman.com

ISBN 978-1-84861-367-6

Copyright © juli Jana 2014

The right of juli Jana to be identified as the author of this work has been asserted by her in accordance with the Copyrights, Designs and Patents Act of 1988. All rights reserved.

definition: a city does not exist until it tells a story

    ecological research: a city has spaces with weeds & butterflies

                the tail of ra-t:
           he did not feare

         the tale of puss–in–boot-s:
              there's a penny to be made

To London once my steppes I bent
Where trouth in no wyse should be faynt
The Taverner took me by the sleve
'Sir' sayeth he 'wyll you your way assay'
                      london lyckpenny

london-town*

        it was puss–in–boot-s that spoke[1]

he jumped up   * in childhood with boots on[2]
thigh high boots, cocky hat * puss–in–boot-s your hat is a-skew

      john goodyear knows you[3]
        looked into your eyes

     they looked rather yello
     eyeing ra-t at waterlo[4]

  puss take off your cape & hat
    the long ostrich feathers & all that
        ;but keep your boots on
          (keep your boots-on
       to stomp with –
         don't drop the look
             the look

you dropped your face
it was left lying in a heap
next to the lamppost
on piccadilly circus
lit up at night   )what year is this then?

footnotes:

(INSTRUCTION: *to be read by a 2nd voice that interrupts the first voice*)

*londinium on the bend of the great river, a great place for trade, for settlement, for ships to anchor

[1] puss knows ra-t well tat-a-tat tell
[2] it is a fluke that I came. fluke- flooking- flood- mud- muddle- muddling- puddle- pud
[3] every year is a good year is what john said
[4] place of great victory &de feat – let ra-t rewrite history a-100 or more years after that

watch out for location. for weariness of prolonged human settlement with its cares
         THERE BE

    WORDTUNNELS

r3

as the new moon landed at the festival of st scholastic in 1242, the tide met the torrents from the river, the fords were impassable so ra-t chose the bank, the banks burst, so ra-t chose the bridge, the bridge was concealed by floods, so ra-t swam past lambeth palace to the mills where he could play with butterflies on a sunny day[1].

it was all gone, the arable land gone with its gardens & the mills with their weirs damaged, the meadows overwhelmed with a rush of water; so ra-t found a plank & drifted with the flow, he let the flow take him to the great palace of westminister, letting it spin him around & around in the lake in the centre in the middle of the hall with boats & persons & twigs & weeds from the banks. the water burst the banks, it burst onto roadways & markets, into cellars & drains, even into palaces   – o the violence of the river thames!

there be more footnotes

¹butterflies
comma ragged outline of wings
camouflage
hibernates in spring
summer dances

painted lady migrates from north africa
at 10 miles per hour
seeks nectar in garden flowers
flight   light   long

holly blue looking to lay eggs
flies flutters march to october
sky reflects   found: shepherd's bush

large white   also known as cabbage white
lays eggs on cabbages
seeks vegetable plots for flight   found: brockley

red admiral   arrives from the continent
chrysalis hangs under nettle leaf
transforms after 17 days   found gardens: islington

common blue   usually brown
lives about three weeks
caterpillars eat clover   found: blackheath

grey-veined white   at blue bell time
first flies in may
prefers wet spots   found: gardens & cemeteries

r5

puss–in–boot-s gingerly circles the edges-of-burnt-out-fires his
boots pulled to knee, walks streets-at-night
ra-t scampers amongst burnt-out-dwellings & glowing embers,
jumps a few remaining walls to view the rising-smoke, the
devastation-of-fires … of fires …   fires [1]

     firecat leaps
                   ra-t scurries out of reach
                                   dusts coat

ra-t wiggles his nose. er . er. a wha.hap.pened to the sul.phur
smell, the fet.id air. twitch, fuddle, funk it is hot. hott.er than
previous summers, but … then the day cometh when the sun
will burn like a furnac-e.

fire fire london town a-burning
pour on water purr on wa-ter!
call the bucket boys, call the bucket boys !
issue twelve new buckets of leather
ring the church bells backwards !
bring on the crimson livery cloth

1 fires of london

an unearthly glow – burning eternally
961 fires from 60 AD to 125 AD
fires continue to rage till one-thousand-and-eighty-seven
watling street, aldersgate, silver street,
cheapside, bread street, wood street
1666 the greatest of all fires, the fire of london
started in the house of the king's baker in pudding lane
mysterious fires in paternoster square light up the city
st. paul's razed to the ground – burning embers
          weeds spring up, yellow edible – *flowers of fire*
city up in flames, never again build in wood
          london bridge is falling down, pour on water, pour on water
1093 – 1220 untold fires throughout london town
royal exchange, guildhall, houses of parliament
some by arson, most by accident
  the noble fire fighters *meir cladde in reede velvette** between
1748 onwards seven-and- a- thirty theatres went up in fire
     iron gates and prison bars melt
     water in wells boil
      fleet river blocked with ash pile up
13 thousand 200 houses razed
89 churches destroyed
the war cry remains *fire! fire*!
O : ring the bells. ring the bells backwards for the city be red. so
many dead.so many dead.all fall down.dance a circle…sing with the
frogs: red dead
*red the cockney slang for gold
the fire-fighters of london wore crimson livery cloth. their
commander died in the fire of 1861 pausing to undo the red silk
paisley kerchief from his neck

r7

ra-t scurries out of reach of each & every fire, the flames, the smoke
but o dear his hair is singed   he settles among weeds & frogs[1]

text… little frogs shelter huddle at lancaster gate hear the influence of leaves weeds in a spot herb-robert redshank iron wall-rocket gate & named bright as light in such thistle-torn cleat (get yourself a small drink for to flower slip-a-lip with oxtip sip celebrate oxalis sprout (sour a poet should write a text with moving cloth & space such is time Signed waste as I *writ* it turned to ashes as the bus came by birds twits flower *naturall as citie* fathers sleep sparrow *traxacum officinale* dandy dandyLion hung where is no date of time for *yeares* or lives in Abrahams bosome sleeps he in fairest pen declare virtues common of weed ((faith works the said elizabeth of virtue over lives chasing pavements of late

the grave *et floret fato non violanda truci* when bones be rot common ragwort sodden for further execution of the letter take Order that all the Words morpheme included Answer there to as above in said Books as in the Sale of Said books as sold in my Warranty published to add an appendix arising from Ashes after 1666 a dictionary of london streets its citizens rents yards buckets of water after a night of hybrid hear *anthem right sun rhyme* sheds blue nightshade slips ships merchants full of plague guy fawkes is no fool though he wears a mask a chicory flower gathers butterflies on demand of historian & Inke & Son & *redivivum* & & & … … Lon:§TON bells from bunHill bang since wind westerly fever

(INSTRUCTION - can be read down and across with or without 2nd voice as an echo, at the same time or one voice following the other)

[1] london weeds

wild-wetness-sprung-unbred
scourge-never-dying-said
cherished-green-oxygen-mint
fire-wrought-afterglow-show
pierce-slag-slab-brick-debri

dandelion drawn-up-nutrient-flow
common-cloth-lion-at-heart
strong-seeded-wound-clock
air-borne-potent-arrow
goldenhead-tortoise-picking
thistle winkle-blue-softest-down
in-spiky-lace-crucifix
collar-worn-straight-hard
spur-stemmed-wooden-grown
lunar-dust-nightly-sworn-nettle
nettle black-jack-sprat-flat
spiked-climber-wind-flower
sun-splashed-yellow-shower
stretched-stalk-hookedseed
vitamin-green-sweet-dream
oxalis oval-cup-buttered-face-sorrel
bending-necks-straggle-straight
year-round-sour-sweet-meat
unmasked-bright-praise-sundrawn
salad-maze-roadside-treat
rocket-green-leaf-chrome-shard
unbred-hard-black-hacked-edge
gold-cup-head-sway
flower-bright-ever-new
bronzed-crown-ribbon-sprung

r11

ra-t scurries past the courts.doors blocked with the dead from
cholera.If it be not fire.it be the black death o for fire to kill off
the spread of disease the bodies piled up the walking death.
he wriggles his back saying I not be a disease carrying rat.I be
ra-t.friend of puss–in–boot-s.puss let's fly to the moon

o the stench! puss–in–boot-s looks for catnips for flowering
yellow rocket after the fires.ra-t chews on london-weeds.basks
in sunspots on stone & rubble weed-seeded[1]

botanical observation: *in the aftermath of the great fire a yellow-
flowering plant known as london fire grew. this be rocket. it grew
even more abundantly on the ruins around st. paul's the following
year and 300 years later outside the city boundaries still.*

r12

(INSTRUCTION:
p-l-e-a-s-e-f-e-e-l-f-r-e-e-t-o-r-e-a-d-i-n-a-n-y-w-h-i-c-h-w-a-y)
(t-w-o-v-o-i-c-e-s-o-v-e-r-l-a-p-p-i-n-g-i-n-t-e-r-j-e-c-t-i-n-g-o-r-t-o-g-e-t-h-e-r)

[1]weeds   london rocket   common groundsel
hawthorn gardens   calcareous soils
     creeping buttercup   london weeds
     sprouting mushroom   acid soil   ashes
     intermittent sun   wall-rocket
     shade   common mouse - ear
     climbing fuschias   chalky soil areas
     morning glory
herb and weed
     tree roots   nutrients of debri   sprouting weeds
     rows of ants   summer light
     long grasses   shepherds purse
creeping thistle
     fat hen   field bindweed
   light   scarlet pimpernel   spear thistle
creeping buttercup   spider webs
   flying moths   slabs and weeds   random weeds
     settle   pigeons squat   herb-robert
   early daffodils   six-spot burnet month   wall-rocket
hedge   birdweed
     grasshopper   cluster yellow flowers at tip
ivy covered lintel   insects hover
ink-cap   plastered walls   spin around   tree framed windows
     grassed sidewalks   climbers
     redshank   yellow bricks
     lesser celandine   intricate
     delicate   common mouse ear
     perennial   london rocket   common
couch
     arable land   tubular seed pods   riddlesdown
common toadflax   ground elder

r13

bells ring out: turn back dick whittington!!turn back!!turn!
puss–in–boot-s pulls the bell ropes swinging from side to side
peers at guildhall stroking his whiskers.sheds a wink…
(he knows who will be mayor next
it be master dick(

twenty-and-four alderman[1] sit in guildhall
                        why spend life waiting o roses[2]
so silky   danger high 1450
                  the city sleeps paradise
mayor & all   trappings on the wall
                     wakes before dawn counting money
               come crow chanticleer crow from borough
market[4]
turn back dick   cook-a-doodle-do
                 hear the bells of london town too
selfishness will settle   churches aspire
      let caxton print a pace   print a page and lace
puss -in- boots smiles at ra-t   open the ports
downstream   docks shall be built
                london pride ever

r14

[1] alder, older, elder be, tree he did do- die-doe so see for time & space for history & race
[2] ring-a ring-a rosies all are dead blackdeath the crows well fed pockets full of money bags full of rye ring-a-ring-a rosies all fall down
[3] paradise lost paradise found what a day in paradise smell the stench grab the wench on the stairs alongside st. pauls remember john donne he was all done for
[4] cock-a-doo-dle-doo buckle-on-his-shoe lord mayor do us a favour don't cut london pride. there shall be a queen still

r15

for in truth the-thames be for swim for trade for buckets of water for ra-t & mates to swim its banks to tunnel finding ways to sewers to gangplanks of anchored boats to the great currency to blessings as puss–in–boot-s feathers his hat & buckles his boots.such boots. such a livelihood

                   blessed be the great th-ames
        ship-s with m-asts   the tide will tur-n
     drin-k dri-nk d-rink
               londeners d-rink . . . .   forgive us
   after the flood   we-beg
            mo-ney mon-ey mone-y
                 lenders are lenders be
    merchants purchase   g o o d s
        g o o d s
                note mayoral rights
      barons lords merchants
  wherefore we will & strictly command that our aforesaid barons
                   of our aforesaid city
  be allowed to trade in all its finery   g o o d s
       liberties   wholly & fully
     appertaining   truly truly shall trade
        horses and kings   three masts
   traitors will be tied on poles in the river to await the tide
        gatekeepers of the city gates
 aldgate moorgate lancaster gate newgate bishops gate cripplegate ludgate
   alderman & gatekeepers of the seven gates hold the key masters of london town   there be an announcement[1]

r16

[1]**latter day announcement : redevelopment of Blackfriars Station with railway bridge(previously named St Pauls station):**
we, the Alderman and Common Councillors for the Ward of Castle Baynard, would be delighted if you could join us, together with representatives of Transport for London and Network Rail, to hear a short presentation of the final proposals for Blackfriars Station, the pedestrian crossings and the timescales involved with the project. the meeting will take place at St. Andrew by the Wardrobe, EC4 at 12 noon, on Friday 9th March 2007

announcement enactment : we, the Alderman and Common Councillors for the Ward of Castle Baynard, are delighted that together with representatives of Transport for London and Network Rail we can announce the completion of the proposals for Blackfriars Station with the sun panels January 2011

) ... *it is I who read this announcement on the bridge, not ra-t. not* puss–in–boot-s . *such changes they made once mor: sun panels for Blackfriars Bridge?*
aforehand ra-t twiddled his whiskers twiddled his tail when there were changes then – a bridge built on arches was such fun, it stemmed the flow of the thames, stopped it freezing over. ra-t & his mates swam in circles, drifted with the reeds from bank to bank. burrowed along the edges, feed on turnips drifting from the market. I'll get back to the story of ra-t ... in a while I'll relate where I spotted him, but first the matter of the market, the verdict and such... (

19

r17

watch out for fires for flood * for freezing * for dropping your face
                        on southbank market
              for ra-t in the bin chewing cab.bage[1]

news of the day:

        on southbank bridge after high tides
            rats do feast
              on traitors heads & carrots [2]

¹ **southbank market**

cabbagE
cab.bage grows in a-cres . in acres . if it were not for snail-s . big cat-e-pillars all-green . gr-een & cle-n covering. a .white . hear-t . No more no . more sickness . forGe-t snails check the lie of the-lan-d . this is layere-d & many si-ded . true, tru-e . some cabBages are blu(e)

beetro0t
r-ed r-ipe groW-ing to earth lying in re-Ality)

asparag
Us neeDle poinTing sof-t ben-ded .
Ti-ps not for te . a tip-s for Me .
In the preParA-tion cu-t of tenderness-s
in the cuTting g-rown in soil-l

fEnnel
herBal & strIngent a . lon-g river craY . wild- wet & gRowing should let but-terflies play . what then yellow was wow ! was yell0wy-brown . adMiral flutterby – stRange not-silk-or-spin . Still
spiders !!! twist. and the d.ay smelt all the w.ay cures
lEEks turn!ps po-tatoes   "TISH" won't y-ou buy my prEtty flow-erS

² traitors be hung on poles opposite the market letting the tide pass twice

r19

fire-cat's-smile-cheeses-to-new-moon-slither. reflects on the-
thames. rats & rats tails! er . er. a wha.happened to the sul.phur
smell the fet.id air. twitch-fuddle-funk it is hot. hot.ter than
previous summers.
but then the day cometh when the sun will burn like a furnace .
not even puss–in–boot-s will sit to sun though he wears a
broad-brimmed hat & cape.

ra-t now scurries past the courts.doors blocked with the dead
from cholera the searing sun.it's an old habit. waiting at the
gate to see if the king comes riding past.ra-t knows there is to
be an execution.will the courts decide? what of the king? run
all the king's men!run all the king's horses!the horses & the
horsemen! humpty-dumpty is going for a fall for to hide in a
bush will be of no-avail.we all agree one-and-all.

ludgate prevents the kings entry (all the gates – moorgate,
aldgate …[1]
        the keeper turns the key
        king & coach
        mayor & aldermen
        writ & date

what's foul	bells toll
fouler will be	it'a a verdict
our beasts and ourselves	for whom the bell tolls
in the city square	fair & square
defiled with blood[2]	

        today & gone
        such feebleness
            o the bitterness if the courts ring the bells[3]

r20

[1]run charles run
no place to hide
stay away from countrymen
hide from the common

the king be caught in a bush
bird-in-the-bush
twitter tell the tale
cromwell reigns
charles II wherefore art thou
what is your crown?
will all the rats drown!

[2]blood-sblood-christ'sblood-bleeding-gone-allgone-bittersblood-
bitterwood
[3]the bells of the-old-bailey ring truly
pass along the condemned there be one more drink
pause and confess at the fountain   take the cup
)there shall be the death of a princess one day   what then old bailey

r21

    twisting whiskers
        whippity-snip-slip
                      such a bugger
                      b-bugge-r   d-rat rat-drat

  he got his whiskers singed
  the tobac-co docks

      smell of smoke smell of ra-t   tobacco smells good
             t o o !g! o o d so-good

  beware of being indulgent   beware of the old bailey[1]
      bequeath a legacy
          river rats & foreign merchants
  pirates up the estuary   ships & slaves

        tobacco plantations & all that
    there be coffee houses   coffee houses in the docks
   such a trade
      coffee houses next to the slave poles

        also lifting poles   loading slips
    drat you ra-t you can jump the gangplank to escape[2]

[1] the old bailey will order the ringing of the bells, then its newgate prison, this be better than the bishop of southwark though he be lord, sir richard whittington gave an endowment for the keepers all

[2] ra-t weighed in the balance

ladies & gentlemen of the jury
have you reached your verdict

guilty! always guilty!
we found droppings amongst the tobacco leaves
pollution   disease can spread
we will have to close down the merchants trade

what is that your verdict
the verdict of the court

yes my lord
bury him in the old churchyard
with the butterflies

what then what of the trade from the plantations
what of london town with its traders

that is a matter for another age
the ice will melt
the ships may only enter
no longer travel up & down the thames
only the barges   the barges my lord

r23

rats & rats tails! it is time to escape once more.the jury could not find you.could not get to the vermin.all rats do hide.what tunnels.what sewers.what alley ways.but today.today it is time to leave.leave the damp dank sewer.
ra-t jumps out into the open.scurries past the courts undetected.

traders place balances so that pennies all weigh the same
    o but who counts   who weighs the outcome

)ra-t will you stay in sewers below running along houses in a row)(will you walk the streets)
      … there be toes to nibble in prison.
        there be heads to impale.thames water lapping
        there be moonshine.

fire-cat's-smile-cheeses-to-new-moon-slither,reflection on thames.the moon cuts chimneys-to-shape against-moonglow, ra-t scampers up high- walls,wiggles tail & whiskers,sees the whole of the moon.it scuttles above rooftops,fire-cat leaps boots & all.[1]

[1]teaser & fire-cat
        (sung by cat stevens)

fire-cat watch out for ra-t
you sit fiddle in hand
on moon sized-like-a-plate
a disc thrown into spac(e)
waitin' to grow

chimneys
get swallow(e)d by
incan
-descent light
blu-whit turning purpl(e)
rolls from the insid(e)

teaser ra-t
you th-rew the moon
dusting london town

r25

I waited for you.no, you waited for me.I said I'd back.said I would tell how I met ra-t. tell a story:

saw him ride down the street. charring cross road on a motorbike. a rat. tail stretched out. balancing body. his whiskers testing the width of the traffic. he weaves in & out. as if he needs to watch out for queen victoria's ratcatcher[1]. red beady eyes strength of sun. head held parallel to body reaching forward. lengthening of each vertebrae. ongoing thrust. disappears around the bend. lights of car from behind sets his fur on fire. is it a london rat?. one who escaped the fires disease verdicts? does he come from the sewers? now racing black cabs. had raced the black death thirteen-and-eighty-four? must have run in-&-and-out of dead bodies. up-and-down walls. into no-man's-land. did he carry flees? having transversed clerkenwell road[2]. turnmill street[3]. viewed the sweating sickness 1528. taken to open sewers. quagmires of the city. not safe on the streets. the houses. such noysome streets[4]. wanted to follow him. ask how he had survived. why was he chancing life. dicing death. had he made a pact with the devil ⊠ he had seen the face of the devil. in the bodies. bodies that lined the streets during the repeats of the black death. black death. had he picked up the feare and trembling? he had survived. he was a rat. a possible carrier of the dreaded disease. now scouring the streets of london. what if more than rat? could he be a prophet? his name is 'ra-t' it was blazed on his leather jacket. I sit in the jazz café. foyles bookshop . look out onto the road. where is the prophet? the one with the hairy cloak. sent to nineveh[5].   why the engraving on a slab behind st. paul' :pray for the people of london? I think I smelt a rat. (ra-t it is) .his coat smells of fire. so many fires. always the fires. but always the weeds surviving — flowers of fire

r26

[1]that time be long gone, so too most of the rats, followed him like the piper of hamelin bright jacket & all , also some children followed — then a gate was built — was it newgate or bishopsgate?

[1]look on the northern edge of clerkenwell green for a well . mystery plays there performed for centuaries – *beyond the memory of man* . just beyond an eleventh century church and hospital , the knights templar and knights hospitaller . in the seventh centuary ralph fitz brian became lord of the fee of clerkenwell within the manor of stepney by knight service . in 1303 the prioress of clerkenwell petitioned Edward I to provide and order a remedy because the people of londiniumn lay waste and destroyed her corn and grass by their miracle plays and wrestling matches ... *for they are a savage folk. even putting to torch the hall and dormitory of the knights, also the counting house, the distillery, the laundry, the slaughterhouse, the stables* . . . the whole of clerkenwell on fire!!! always fires.yes. o synfulle citie! 7 sins in all in al:. thieving ...
c-l-e-r-k-e-n-w-e-l-l-t-h-e-r-e-f-g-e-f-o-r-t-h-e-o-u-t-c-a-s-t-h-e –p-r-o-s-t-i-t-u-t-e-t-h-e-b-e-g-g-a-r: *p-l-e-a-s-e-d-o-n-t-w-h-i-p-t-h-e-w-h-o-a-r-e-!m-a-y-s-h-e-k-e-e-p-h-e-r-f-a-c-e-o-n.* KIND HARTES DREAME. *a thymee to dreamme o synfulle citie!* it be a harbouring house for *masterless men and for such as lyve by thiefte and other such lyke sheefts*

[2]turnmill street near the mills of the current fleet became salubrious under threat from *filth and ordure and rubbage.* there always be cock alley for those who boast of length. one wlliam the parchmenter in 1414 harboured the lollard, sir john oldcastle and was hanged and quartered for his hospitality. what then of jesuits, papists, italians, quakers, brownists, familists, schismatics? – persecute! persecute! persecute! hang & quarer . weeds do come up. also butterflies

[3]noysome with a degree of nastiness unimaginable. there be weeds and there be weeds.

[5]jonah sent to nineveh never forgot the fish . kept blaming god for not sending fire.maybe that's why london got meted out fires. watch out for a whale in the thames!!!says historian watch out for being swallowed

r27

        one two buckle my shoe
     puss–in–boot-s adjust the strap
          cock the hat for barter * for trading
               as a matter-of-fact
  there will be buying-&-selling * trading-&-stocks
                     bowler hat & pointy shoes

  wow the whole of soho nostalgic[1]
  big daddy died . . . . stark naked they cried
      with the rain on cobblestones pitter-pitter-pat
       shoulder to shoulder those with masks those without

ladies & gentlemen get flushed with gin go down town
         see there's pantomime & jugglers in the street
  note high heels drive hard
      up fleet street & turning left   the judge resides

         . . . .

new row, covent gardens[2]. we had soup yesterday
strong with rocket[3] and thyme[4].
today we'll go to the patisserie for bread. ah crumbs!
          watch out for ra-t
you might him catch him)s-niffing
avoid the coffee houses . . .
       no costa coffee as they avoid tax
watch out for [5]…

rats and rats tails! have your boots on & comb your whiskers
puss remember your face

r28

¹soho the place where the porno king died in 2007 leaving a fortune but what of the ladies of the night in the street the shadows. do cry all but not for the people's princess nor whisper her name
²no one knows who made the covenant. could be ra-t and pussy-boots
³rocket to be found anywhere in london: parks, backyards, churchyards, forgotten gardens, between slabs
⁴thyme is a gentle flavour but then time is the opposite though year can be good year
⁵watch out for location. for weariness of prolonged human settlement with its cares and woes

botanical observation: in the aftermath of the great fire a yellow-flowering plant known as *london fire* grew. a yellow-flowering plant known as *flowers of fire* grew in the aftermath of the great fire of london. known as *yellow rocket* a yellow-flowering plant grew in the aftermath of the great fire of london. *london rocket* a yellow-flowering plant grew in the aftermath of the great fire of london. *flower of fire* a yellow flowering plant grew in the aftermath of the great fire of london

last note:
weeds there be.food for ra-t.play things also butterflies & all that.

ra-t did not drop his face
   got goggles & a motorbike)) THERE BE ROADS besides tunnels

caution:
watch out for fires.for floods next.for wordtunnels!
   there be black umbrellas to the rescue((don't tell puss–in–boot-s
   don't tell boris johnson   do tell ra-t

www.ingramcontent.com/pod-product-compliance
Lightning Source LLC
Chambersburg PA
CBHW021949040426
42448CB00008B/1310